SECRETS OF PRAYING

HEAVEN &EARTH

TOGETHER

PENNY RIDDLE

Tulsa, OK

21 20 19 18 17   10 9 8 7 6 5 4 3 2 1

Secrets of Praying Heaven and Earth Together
ISBN: 978-1-68031-179-2
Copyright © 2017 by Penny Riddle

Published by Harrison House Publishers
P.O. Box 35035
Tulsa, Oklahoma 74153
www.harrisonhouse.com

In loving memory of my grandmother, Sylvia Patterson,
and all of my aunts and uncles
who have moved on to their reward.

Also in dedication to all who remain:
my mother, Joyce Bagwill;
my Aunts Rosie, Carol, and Shirley;
and my Uncle Darrell.

Endorsement

I always loved to hear my dad, Kenneth E. Hagin, talk about Sister Sylvia Patterson. He always referred to her as the little redheaded lady that could pray heaven and earth together.

I loved hearing about the supernatural happenings that he attributed to Sister Sylvia's praying. I remember my dad saying he had never seen the supernatural in such display anywhere else as when he was pastoring in Farmersville, Texas. Sister Sylvia and her prayer group prayed earnestly over every prayer request and there was testimony after testimony of many miracles.

Pastor Penny Riddle is Sister Sylvia's granddaughter. Penny was an eyewitness of her grandmother's prayer life.

I believe this book will be a great inspiration for praying people to press in and expect more of the supernatural in their lives.

Don't miss reading this book! It is a wonderful privilege to be a praying person working with God for the supernatural.

Dr. Pat Hagin Harrison

Contents

Acknowledgments

I would like to thank several people who made this book possible.

First my husband, Rick, and our daughters and their husbands, Rebecca and Jason Hogan and Rachel and Jacob Guzman. Thank you for encouraging me every day that I could do this, and that it would make a difference in the world. Your love and support and prayer were always there.

Thanks to my mom and Aunt Rosie for all of your knowledge about Grandma; also my sisters and cousins whose input into the book has made it better.

Also Mary Hughes for all of the stories of my grandmother, especially the ones about her praying for Mary's son Henry Tackett, and her sister, Sammy Patterson.

Thank you to LaVerne Adekunle for helping me type this up the right way and to Laurie Grey for helping me to even start the book.

Thank you, Pat Harrison, for always honoring us and showing us the same love you showed my grandmother.

And thank you, Mrs. Billye Brim, for helping me to make this book a reality, for believing in me, and for loving my grandmother the way I did. I hope to one day be an anointed writer just like you.

Foreword

Dr. Billye Brim

"The little redheaded woman who could pray heaven and earth together," was how Dr. Kenneth E. Hagin always referred to her. And refer to her he did! One of the most amazing stories he told about this seasoned prayer warrior was the vision she had of a woman who had disappeared as a teenaged girl from her small Texas town of Farmersville and was presumed dead, kidnapped and murdered by a motorcycle gang.

In fact, Brother Hagin often told of the supernatural things that happened in the Farmersville church he pastored. He said he'd never seen them so prolifically demonstrated anywhere else. He attributed that in large part to the prayer group led by Sister Sylvia Patterson. He often said, "If you wanted something, you'd better be sure you really wanted it before you turned it over to that group because they would get it."

On one of her visits to Kenneth Hagin's Annual Summer Campmeeting at the Tulsa Civic Center in the 1980s, Kenneth and Oretha Hagin invited Patsy Behrman (now Cameneti) and me to listen in as they recalled "old times" with Sister Sylvia. Oh my! What a blessing it was to hear them talk about the miracles at Farmersville and Sister Sylvia's prayer part in them.

They laughed as they recalled how once when the Hagins were driving to church, they saw Sister Sylvia walking down the road wearing her bathrobe. Her husband had forbidden her to go to church and had hidden her clothes. Not to be stopped, she just donned her robe and headed toward church. The Hagins picked her up and turned around and went back to their place where Oretha gave her some clothes to wear.

Pastor Penny Riddle is Sister Sylvia's granddaughter, and I encouraged her to write about this amazing woman's prayer life so it would inspire present-day praying people to enter into and expect more of the supernatural. Penny's aunts (Sylvia Patterson's daughters) came with the Riddles to our Sunday prayer at Prayer Mountain in the Ozarks and shared how they often trailed along behind their mother like so many ducklings as she walked to church and to prayer meetings, and how they experienced the supernatural at their mother's side. Penny too was an eyewitness and recipient of her beloved grandmother's prayer life.

You don't want to miss this book. I plan to promote it wherever I share on the privilege of working with God in prayer. Sister Sylvia Patterson did just that. She worked with the Creator!

(1)

My Grandmother's Secrets

In a lot of ways, my Grandma Sylvia's story isn't very different from the stories of other people who had grown up in the rural Southwest with little means during hard times. She was born in 1913, the third of eight children, to a farmer and his wife in the small community of Merit, Texas. She grew up a strong-willed little redhead who pushed a plow and picked cotton when she wasn't in school or doing chores. Never in her childhood did she have more than two dresses and one pair of shoes.

At 18 years old, she married a man who was ten years her senior and went on to raise nine of her own children in a two-bedroom house with a kerosene stove and no plumbing. Her life was never easy, but it was good. She made it that way.

And by the time she had died, she had left all of her children, grandchildren, and great grandchildren something extremely valuable; something far more valuable than if she had been a billionaire. She left us a legacy of prayer, one that has blessed every area of our family.

That's what made my grandmother different from so many of her generation, even among Christians. She had a very real relationship with God. She communed with Him constantly and relied on Him in every situation. She put her faith in Him alone and when she called, God answered every time. Her prayers were so powerful that one minister, Brother Hagin, called her "the little redhead who could pray heaven and earth together." In other words, she was a woman who knew how to get what she (and other people) needed from God.

Although my grandmother grew up in a Christian home, she didn't give her life to Jesus and start to church until after her twins boys, Aubrey and Audrey, were born. They were her second pregnancy, born in July of 1935. One of the twins however, Audrey, only lived a short time, and Aubrey was so small (about two pounds), he almost died also. My grandmother was devastated! It was then she told the Lord that if He would save Aubrey, then she would serve Him all the days of her life. And from the day she told that to God, she always kept her promise and lived a life of faith. She believed and practiced every word in the Bible that she understood.

Aubrey was so small that Sylvia had to feed him with an eye dropper. She had to be with him constantly and prayed over him all the time, standing on Psalms 118:17, "I shall not die, but live, and declare the works of the Lord." Her mother-in-law told her, "Why don't you just let him die? He is too small."

Sylvia said, "No! I won't do that. He will live and not die!" She thanked God daily that Aubrey was growing stronger and stronger. And he did. He grew into a healthy child, and my grandmother gave God all the glory.

From that time, her life changed. She quit going to dances with her husband. She went to church every time it was open and got involved in all the prayer meetings at the church and in the home groups. As her family grew, she always took the kids with her. She never let anything stop her from going. When she was home, she would spend her days praying and thanking the Lord. Some of my earliest memories are of Grandma Sylvia working in the kitchen — canning tomatoes, pickles, and beets, shucking corn, snapping peas — and her praying and singing the entire time.

It was a wonderful way to grow up, seeing my grandmother praying and being thankful all the time, and my mother is the same way. So am I, and it is something my children and grand-children see me do. I realize, not only did Grandma Sylvia leave a legacy of prayer to her daughters, but I see it in me and in my two daughters. By the age of three, both of them had Jesus in their hearts and had received their prayer language, and if some-one was hurt or sick they began to pray for them, even at that age. Now *my* grandson Jeraden, asked Jesus into his heart when he was three. I know beyond a shadow of a doubt, my grandma's legacy will continue to pass down for many generations to come.

Although the name of this book is *Secrets of Praying Heaven and Earth Together*, my grandmother's secrets aren't really secrets at all. Everything she said and did came from the scriptures. These are things that anyone can do and get the same kind of results my family still does. I share them with you here knowing that, if you'll put these "secrets" to practice, you will also get the same kind of results: answers to your prayers every time you pray.

$$\left(\,2\,\right)$$

Make Time for God

Every time I would go to see my grandmother, I always thought she had company. When I would go up to the door, I could hear her talking.

I'd knock and walk in. "Hi Grandma. Is someone here?"

"Just me, Jesus and the Holy Ghost!" she'd say. Then she'd start shouting and dancing. That happened all the time. No, my grandmother wasn't crazy! She just understood that a successful prayer life was fueled by an active relationship with God.

What does it mean to have a relationship with God? It means spending time with Him on a daily basis. John 10:27 (AMP) says: "The sheep that are My own hear My voice and listen to Me; I know them, and they follow Me." How can you hear Him if you don't spend time with him? The answer is you can't. You have to spend time with someone to get to know them, and in a relationship with God that means spending time in the Word.

If we are so busy and distracted by the cares of this world and we don't spend time with Him, we can't hear what God is saying to us. Mark 4:19 tells us the worries of this life, the deceitfulness of wealth and the desire for other things come in and choke the Word, making it unfruitful. We have to stop letting things like strife, bitterness, hatred, and hurt feelings dominate us. We have to wake up, stir ourselves and spend time in the presence of the Lord.

This is not always easy, but it is the only way to keep God working in your life. In 1 Samuel 30:6, it says, "And David was greatly distressed; for the people spake of stoning him, because the soul of all the people was grieved, every man for his sons and for his daughters: but David encouraged himself in the Lord his God." It must have been very difficult for David to turn to God during this time. His men were ready to kill him! But instead of staying distressed, he spent time with God and sought His counsel. This brought great victory for David and his men. But David would have never had that victory if he had not spent time with God.

One of my grandmother's favorite scriptures was 2 Chronicles 7:14: "If my people, which are called by my name, shall humble themselves, and pray, and seek my face, and turn from their wicked ways; then will I hear from heaven, and will forgive their sin, and will heal their land." One day while I was working, this scripture kept coming up in my Spirit. I could hear Grandma Sylvia saying it almost like she was right in the room!

My response to that was, "Yes Lord, I remember her saying this scripture to me."

Then the Lord said, "Penny, if *you*, who are called by my name (and I knew He was talking both to me and to the body of Christ) shall humble yourselves, and pray, and seek my face — not a little, but seek me daily through prayer and the Word and worship and really press in — and pray and turn from the things of this world, then you, Penny, and the body of Christ, will hear from heaven!" In other words, we have to seek God daily and throughout each day. *Only then* can we hear exactly what He is saying and *only then* can He answer our prayers.

Someone once asked my grandmother, "What was the difference in the way you prayed and the way we pray today?" She answered: "People today are praying ten to fifteen minutes and expecting God to jump with an answer. We stayed on our knees in the church praying until God said, 'It's done.'" She knew getting answers from God required time in His presence. There were many times when she would pray until one or two in the morning because she would not stop until she knew she had gotten her answer. When Jesus told her it was done, she knew it was done. And when it was done, she would dance around saying, "Thank you, Jesus! Thank you, Jesus! I know, I know, I know it's done. Hallelujah!" Then, sure as you know, the answer to her prayers would come.

This was something she learned as a young mother. One time her cookstove quit working, and they didn't have money for another one. So she said, "Lord, you know I need a cookstove." Then she took the time and prayed until she knew it was on the way. Then one of her boys who was just coming in from outside told her someone had dumped some things in a nearby ditch, and it looked like there was a cookstove down there! So she told her boys to get it and bring it back home. Not only did it look better than the stove they had before, they hooked it up, and every burner and the oven worked perfectly. Things like that always happened for my grandma.

Just because my grandmother spent time with God doesn't mean she was on her knees all the time. She had nine children which means she was working from the time her feet hit the floor until the time her head hit the pillow! She would get up early and do what Matthew 6:33 said and seek first God's kingdom. She would start praying for her family while she cooked her husband and children breakfast. Once everyone had eaten, she would start cleaning up the kitchen, singing and praying the whole time. No matter what she was doing around the house she'd sing and pray every day, all day.

She had a direct line to the Father because she always made time for God. She had learned that when you get to know God, you can fully trust and rely on Him. The more time you spend with Jesus, the more you can trust Him. And that trust is faith.

In Luke 17:6 (AMP) it says: "And the Lord said, "If you have [confident, abiding] faith in God [even as small] as a mustard seed, you could say to this mulberry tree [which has very strong roots], 'Be pulled up by the roots and be planted in the sea'; and [if the request was in agreement with the will of God] it would have obeyed you. " In Luke 8:25 (AMP), Jesus "said to them, 'Where is your faith (your confidence in Me)?' They were afraid and astonished, saying to one another, 'Who then is this, that He commands even the winds and the sea, and they obey him?'" When we trust Him, we develop that confidence that whatever we ask, have need of, or command, He is going to bring it to pass.

Spending time with God isn't always about studying and praying and reading. It's also about listening so we can hear from heaven (2 Chron. 7:14). Matthew 24:25 (AMP) says: "Listen carefully, I have told you in advance." As believers, we have to listen carefully to the voice of God. He is always trying to tell us things in advance. John 10:27 (AMP) says, "The sheep that are my own hear my voice and listen to me; I know them, and they follow me." But if we are too busy and not listening, we don't know where to go or what's coming, and we can miss the divine connections God has put in place to answer our prayers.

God is not asking us to give up anything by spending more time with Him; He's asking us to go deeper with Him. He wants to bless us and answer our prayers, but we have to get into His presence and His Word. As we constantly seek Him and that trust comes, we then have to be willing to listen and obey.

(3)

Know and Do the Word

My grandmother had a real revelation of the connection between the Word and prayer. She believed that if someone would get into the Word, know it, and do what it said, the blessing would be there and prayers would be answered. That's how she lived.

Just like 2 Timothy 2:15 says, my grandmother knew a believer was to "study to shew thyself approved unto God, a workman that needeth not to be ashamed, rightly dividing the word of truth." She had her favorite scriptures marked in her Bible so she could study them whenever possible, but she would also keep them on her refrigerator, so she could read them all the time!

Grandma Sylvia would say, "Whatever you are going through, maybe sickness, get your scriptures out to stand on them. Place them where you can read them. Every time you walk by them, say them out loud. Then remind the Lord what He said in His Word." She stood on 1 Peter 2:24, that by Jesus stripes, she was healed. She would say, "I'm already healed. I take my healing now!" "Read the scriptures out loud," she'd always say, "so the devil knows you mean business, and he cannot take it from you."

There was not one scripture in the Bible that my Grandma Sylvia did not trust would come to pass. She believed in every word. If Jesus said something, she took Him at His Word and acted on it no matter what it looked like in the natural.

I can still hear what she would say over and over again: "Use your faith. That just means you trust God when He says He is going to do something." She stood on Matthew 21:22, "And all things, whatsoever ye shall ask in prayer, believing, you shall receive."

Not only did Grandma Sylvia know the Word and believe it, she did it, just like it says in James 5:22–25:

> But be doers of the word, and not hearers only, deceiving yourselves. For if anyone is a hearer of the word and not a doer, he is like a man observing his natural face in a mirror; for he observes himself, goes away, and immediately forgets what kind of man he was. But he who looks into the perfect law of liberty and continues in it, and is not a forgetful hearer but a doer of the work, this one will be blessed in what he does.

Hearing the Word is vital, so is studying it, but then you have to lay hold of the Word of God to put it to practice. If you're not a doer of the Word, then you are just a good notetaker, and there will be no results. Provision and healing and anything else you have need of comes from obedience to the Word.

Obedience to what God is saying does not only involve obeying the Bible. Throughout my years in ministry, people have come to me and said the Lord was telling them to do a certain thing in the ministry, but they never actually did any of it. They always had some kind of excuse on why they had not done it yet. Some of them never got to fulfill what the Lord told them to do because they passed away.

Don't be the one God tells to do something and you never do it. This is a sure way to not get your prayers answered! Instead, make sure you're the first to say, "Yes Lord," and put your hands to it. Then you can watch God move on your behalf.

In my mind even as a child, I understood that my grandmother's answered prayers were connected to her doing the Word. One Bible principle she believed in was sowing and reaping. Just like a farmer plants a seed and gets a harvest, people reap what they sow. She taught her children the importance of this principle, especially when it came to tithing and, as a result, even her children who weren't serving God at the time were blessed.

Earlier in her life when her husband would give her money, she would always take out some to pay her tithes. She knew if she did this, every time she prayed, the answer would be there, and it was! There was one time, she told God, "Lord, we're out of groceries again, and I don't have any money. I need at least ten dollars to get groceries." Then she got dressed, put on her heels, and went into town by faith. She knew the Lord would provide. Just as she's walking into the store, she found ten dollars in cash. After she praised the Lord and gave Him thanks, she said, "Lord, I should have asked for one hundred dollars. I know you would have let me find that too!" Then she laughed.

Anytime she needed groceries, she would trust God, and people (and even dogs) would put things on her front porch. They never went without groceries. God was always faithful!

Today, people say, "I don't think we are required to tithe. I am no longer under the law." My answer to that is what the Bible says: You are not under the law, but you are under a curse if you rob from God! Malachi 3:8–10 says plainly:

> Will a man rob God? Yet ye have robbed me. But ye say, Wherein have we robbed thee? In tithes and offerings. Ye are cursed with a curse: for ye have robbed me, even this whole nation. Bring ye all the tithes into the storehouse, that there may be meat in mine house, and prove me now herewith, saith the Lord of hosts, if I will not open you the windows of heaven, and pour you out a blessing, that there shall not be room enough to receive it."

Also in Hebrews 7:5–7 (AMP) it says,

> It is true that those descendants of Levi who are charged with the priestly office are commanded in the Law to collect tithes from the people—which means, from their kinsmen—though these have descended from Abraham. But this person [Melchizedek] who is not from their

Levitical ancestry received tithes from Abraham and blessed him who possessed the promises [of God]. Yet it is beyond all dispute that the lesser person is always blessed by the greater one.

So if you want blessing in your life, the best thing to do is obey God and tithe. There is such a joy when you trust God. It's not a chore, it is a pleasure. He has your very best interest at heart.

Another scripture my grandmother believed and practiced was Proverbs 19:17: "He that hath pity upon the poor lendeth unto the Lord; and that which he hath given will he pay him again."

Most country people didn't have much, especially around the time of the Depression. This included my grandmother. One day a disheveled hobo came by my grandmother's house as she was working in the yard.

"Do you have any scissors, ma'am?"

"Yes," she said, going into the house and getting them. "They're a little dull, but you're more than welcome to use them."

The man went over by the tree and started cutting his own hair. Then he brought the scissors back and thanked her.

My grandmother then asked, "Are you hungry? I can fix you something to eat." The man said he was, so she went into the house and fixed him a biscuit and egg sandwich.

That man went back to the railroad and told the other hobos that there was a lady named Sylvia who would feed them if they would go to her back door. After that, many hobos showed up and asked her if she had anything they could eat. Although she didn't have a lot, she would always go and fix them something, usually a biscuit and eggs.

Sylvia believed if hungry people came by her house, it was the Lord bringing them by. She made sure she took care of everyone that came to her door because she believed Hebrews 13:2: "Be not forgetful to entertain strangers: for thereby some have entertained angels unawares."

My grandmother loved serving people. She would do just what Psalm 100:2 said, "Serve the Lord with gladness: come before his presence with singing." Every time someone would come, she would sing and dance around saying, "Thank you Jesus, thank you Jesus" because she knew the Lord sent them and she always had something to feed them, even when sometimes it didn't look like it in the natural.

Sometimes it was like the little widow lady in 1 Kings 17:10-15:

> So he arose and went to Zarephath, and when he came to the gate of the city, behold, the widow woman was there gathering of sticks: and he called to her, and said, fetch me, I pray thee, a little water in a vessel, that I may drink. And as she was going to fetch it, he called to her, and said, Bring me, I pray thee, a morsel of bread in thine hand. And she said, As the Lord thy God liveth, I have not a cake, but a handful of meal in a barrel, and a little oil in a cruse: and, behold, I am gathering two sticks, that I may go in and dress it for me and my son, that we may eat it,

and die. And Elijah said unto her, Fear not; go and do as thou hast said: but make me thereof a little cake first, and bring it unto me, and after make for thee and for thy son. For thus saith the Lord God of Israel, the barrel of meal shall not waste, neither shall the cruse of oil fail, until the day that the Lord sendeth rain upon the earth. And she went and did according to the saying of Elijah: and she, and he, and her house, did eat many days.

No matter how little she had, people were always welcome at her house.

Here's the thing. My grandma never let the cares of this life come in and choke out the Word of God. It didn't matter what she had or didn't have or what was going on, she was always in His presence. There was never a time that I can remember that my grandmother was not praying, praising, or in the Word, and it made her strong in Him.

Another scripture in the Bible my grandmother was obedient to was allowing herself to be led by the Holy Spirit (Romans 8:14). If the Holy Spirit prompted her to do something, she'd do it, and great things would happen.

One particular time, the Lord used her in the gifts of tongues on a Sunday morning. A couple visiting from another country happened to be driving by the church, and they decided to come into the service. During the service, the Lord told Grandma Sylvia, "I want you to give them a word in tongues." She did, yet there was no interpretation. Afterwards the man and his wife came up to my grandmother and said, "I didn't know you could speak our language!"

My grandmother had no idea what he was talking about. The man said, "You spoke our language perfectly! I understood every word you just spoke. It was a word just for us." It made my grandmother so blessed when the Holy Spirit used her this way!

I would have to say that of all the scriptures my grandmother lived by, one of the most important was Ephesians 6:18, "Praying always with all prayer and supplication in the Spirit, being watchful to this end with all perseverance and supplication for all the saints." She especially prayed in the Spirit all the time, even during church. By the time we were pastors of Step of Faith church (for five years), she really couldn't hear very well, and so she would quietly pray in tongues. And sometimes she would just start laughing and praising the Lord. If it was anyone else, it might have been disruptive. But when Grandma Sylvia laughed and praised, it ushered in the Holy Spirit, and everyone got blessed.

(4)

Be Committed

My son, do not forget my teaching, But let your heart keep my commandments; For length of days and years of life [worth living] and tranquility and prosperity [the wholeness of life's blessings] they will add to you. Do not let mercy and kindness and truth leave you [instead let these qualities define you]; Bind them [securely] around your neck, write them on the tablet of your heart. So find favor and high esteem in the sight of God and man. Trust in and rely confidently on the Lord with all your heart and do not rely on your own insight or understanding. In all your ways know and acknowledge and recognize Him, and He will make your paths straight and smooth [removing obstacles that block your way].

Proverbs 3:1–6 (AMP)

My grandmother's commitment to God and His Word spread to every area of her life. That included her family and her church, and that commitment is another key to why her prayers were so successful.

One of the most memorable stories about my grandmother's commitment to church was from when she was a young. She never let anything or anybody keep her out of church, not even her husband, and he tried many times.

My grandfather, JD, was not always good to my grandmother. One time before Sunday evening church, he hid her shoes from her to keep her going. So my grandma put on her galoshes and went to church anyway. When she got there, she testified: "The devil tried to stop me from coming to church tonight, but bless God, I'm here anyway!" Then she started shouting and dancing!

So the next time, my grandfather took all of her clothes outside and burned them. But that didn't stop her either! She put on her house coat, got the children dressed, and off they went walking down the road, like a mother duck with her little ducklings following her. To make matters worse, my grandfather drove by them in the car, honking and waving.

"Mom, there goes Daddy honking and waving at us," one of her children said.

"Don't pay any attention to your dad," she said calmly. "We can so do this without him."

Thankfully her pastors, Brother and Sister Hagin, were driving by and noticed Sylvia did not have her dress on. They picked her and the children up and took them to the parsonage where Sister Hagin got a dress for Sylvia to wear to church. Once again, Sylvia got up and testified how the devil tried and lost again! And she was like that her whole life. Regardless of what happened, my grandmother always got to church to get in the manifest presence of the Lord!

I think this is one area where so many believers are missing it today. They are so quick to have an excuse not go to church. They just give in to all sorts of excuses instead of getting to the very place they need to be to hear from God. My grandmother truly believed Philippians 4:13 (AMP), "I can do all things [which He has called me to do] through Him who strengthens *and* empowers me [to fulfill His purpose—I am self-sufficient in Christ's sufficiency; I am ready for anything and equal to anything through Him who infuses me with inner strength and confident peace.]" She used that scripture to help her stay committed.

My grandmother was also committed to her family, even my grandfather. She prayed for him daily and did he change for the better fast? No, he didn't. It took 32 years for my grandfather to give his life to the Lord, but she stayed determined to love him and committed to pray for him. Because of her faithfulness, he will now spend eternity in the kingdom of God!

Even when some of her children were not serving the Lord, she never gave up on them, and believe me, there was plenty of opportunity. But she always saw the good in them, and when people would try and say bad about any of her family, she would say, "No, they are saved and serving the Lord." And when people would point out the bad things they were doing, she would only say, "The Lord promised me my household, so they are saved!" Her confession was always the Word.

That's what we believers have to do too. We have to consistently let the Word be final authority in our lives, no matter the circumstances. Grandma would consistently say the Lord promised her household would be saved before they died, and every one of them were all born again. Those of her living children and grandchildren all have personal relationships with Jesus because she never gave up on any of them.

Grandma taught all of us to never give up on people, to always walk in love and to always pray. When I was young, I would go with her and my mother to prayer meetings that started before church and, many times, would go on until midnight. This kind of commitment has yielded amazing results in my family, especially in my own father.

My mother's situation with my father was similar to that of my grandmother's. My dad had been to church some when he was younger, but not so much as an adult. He really did not have a relationship with Jesus. And just like my grandfather, my dad would go out and drink on the weekends and then come home late and be not so nice to my mom. Mom would have a prayer cloth prayed over at church by the prayer group and put a piece of it in his billfold and pin part of it in his pillow case. She was determined for him to get saved and serve God.

At one point before I was born, things had gotten so hard that my mom wanted to give up on her marriage. But God told her to write down all of my father's good traits and bad traits, and she realized the good outweighed the bad! Then God told her that if she would take her hand off my dad, He would take care of it.

And God did! When I was young, my mom's pastor, Brother Goforth, would come by and talk to my dad about the Lord. My mom would have him over to eat after church, and even though my dad did not like it, he let him come to the house. One Saturday, Brother Goforth saw my dad out in the field hauling hay. He again started talking to him about coming to church. My dad said, "I tell you what. If you will help me get all this hay hauled, I will come to church in the morning." Brother Goforth left, and my dad said, "Good! Got rid of him. He won't be back." But a half hour later, Brother Goforth drove up wearing overalls and said, "Okay, what do you want me to do?" Much to my dad's surprise, Brother Goforth got in there and helped him get it all done.

So the next morning, my dad got up and got dressed for church. My mom said, "What are you doing?" Dad said, "Well, I promised the pastor if he would help me haul hay, I would go to church." And he did! At some point soon after, my father asked Jesus in his heart. He still had a problem cussing, but he did stop drinking, and I only remember my dad saved. He was and is the best dad a child could ever have, especially when Jesus became lord of his life.

My dad got so committed to going to church, that one time, we had some relatives that started visiting us on Sunday mornings. They knew we went to church, but for some reason, they always showed up on a Sunday morning. The first time we stayed at home from church to visit with them, but then my dad said,

"If they come on a Sunday morning again, we are still going to church." Well they came again, and my dad said, "Well, y'all can stay here or go with us to church, and if you are not coming along, we'll see you after." Well, they hadn't even thought about it being a Sunday, and they didn't want to go, so we got dressed and went and left them at the house! They never came back on a Sunday.

Today, not only is my dad saved and a man of God, he is an ordained minister, all because my mom wouldn't give up on him.

It's like my grandmother would always tell me: "Whatever you start, finish it. Be faithful to what God has called you to do, stay focused on God, and He will always move on your behalf!"

$$\text{(5)}$$

Maintain Peace and Joy

Grandma Sylvia loved to sing songs with scriptures in them, and one of her favorites was from Isaiah 55:12 (AMP):

For you will go out [from exile] with joy And be led forth [by the LORD HIMSELF] WITH PEACE; The mountains and the hills will break forth into shouts of joy before you, And all the trees of the field will clap their hands.

That scripture so described my grandmother. She had so much peace and joy, she was always bursting with it, always laughing and thanking the Lord for everything good in her life. She was happy all the time! That's because she knew how to be happy even when the everything around her seemed to be falling apart.

Most Christians tend to show people when they are going through tough times by talking about their problems and being depressed. Grandma Sylvia's philosophy was this: Never let the devil know he is getting to you; never let him see you cry or defeated, and then you will always win." That's why she would always be laughing and dancing. So no one around her ever knew she even went through trials. When she was going through something, she never told anyone except the Lord, and the Lord would hear her cry and give her peace and joy.

Another scripture in Isaiah says, "You will keep in perfect and constant peace the one whose mind is steadfast [that is, committed and focused on You—in both inclination and character], because he trusts and takes refuge in You [with hope and confident expectation]" (Isaiah 26:3 AMP). Notice that the scripture says constant peace for the mind that is steadfast on God. That was how Grandma did it. She was all the time in perfect and constant peace because she was always in fellowship with God. So if you need peace in your life, that is the scripture you need to stand on. Another scripture like it is in Psalm 119:165 (AMP), "Those who love Your law have great peace; Nothing makes them stumble."

My grandmother believed in stirring up joy. She would say, "Lord, I stir up the joy of the Lord inside of me because Nehemiah 8:10 says, "The joy of the Lord is *my* strength" (emphasis mine). Think about that. He gave us the joy of the Lord as our strength. His *own* joy! Then she would go into Psalms 30:5, "Weeping may endure for a night, but joy comes in the morning." She also taught us it was okay to cry, as long as we didn't stay there.

You know, the church in general needs their laughter back. Maybe you need your laughter back! Right now, just stir that joy up on the inside of you. Put your hands on your stomach and say, "I stir up that joy right now in the name of Jesus." Then just start laughing. At first, your body might not feel like laughing. But if you will start out in faith laughing, then out of your spirit the joy and laughter will come, and then you can't stop! It is amazing when this happens because you can start seeing in the Spirit what God has and wants for you.

We have to see ourselves victorious, not defeated. We have to see ourselves through the eyes of Jesus, and never see ourselves the way we are now. The devil is a liar and the father of it.

Another one of grandmother's favorite scriptures along this line was Psalm 118:24, which says, "This is the day which the Lord hath made; we *will* rejoice and be glad in it" (emphasis mine). Remember that God is the one who created us and we are fearfully and wonderfully made. He sent us His only begotten son, Jesus, for our salvation, healing, prosperity, and anything else we have need of. Jesus paid the price for it all! That should make you want to jump up, shout, and thank the Lord for His goodness and mercy!

But it goes further than that. Philippians 4:4 says, "Rejoice in the Lord always, and again I say rejoice." Grandma Sylvia had this down pat! I never saw her without joy. And if someone else was sad or upset when they ran into Grandma, by the time they left, those bad feelings had turned to joy. It was like she was contagious with happiness.

The Bible tells us that joy is vital in our lives. It's where our strength is built up on the inside. Depression can't come if we are constantly in prayer and stirring up the joy to draw out our strength.

She used to tell me, "Remember to stir up joy. It will come as soon as you say it," and it always did. Even today, if some trial tries to drag me down, I will say, "Thank you, Lord for my joy. I know it is my strength. I stir it up right now." Then I just start getting so happy. Sometimes the spirit of laughter hits me and the presence of the Lord overtakes me.

One thing about my grandmother, she would start singing and dancing around and then she would start saying "Jesus, Jesus, Jesus, Jesus," over and over again. And she prayed in the Spirit all the time. That's what kept her from being in fear or being defeated. She knew Jesus would carry her through anything she was doing or going through. One Sunday night in her younger years, she got up on the alter — it ran from one side of the platform to the other — danced in the Spirit all the way from one side to the other with her eyes closed! She never even stumbled. And when the Spirit left her, she just stepped down and went back to her seat.

If you need mountains moved or joy in your life, if you will just start dancing around in the Spirit, and saying Jesus over and over again, I'm telling you, the whole atmosphere will change, and things will began to move in the Spirit.

There is power in the name of Jesus. Use His name! It is there to use, so use it. And be bold about it. Sinners are not ashamed of using bad language or acting wild, so why should we be ashamed to rejoice about the goodness of God? Grandma Sylvia certainly wasn't.

$$\textcircled{6}$$

Pray Practical Prayers

In case I haven't made it clear so far, my grandmother was extremely practical. So were her prayers. When I say prayer, I don't mean religious prayer, but Bible-based, Spirit-led prayer. And when she wasn't praying scriptures, she was praying in tongues.

Grandma Sylvia believed the first step to getting prayers answered was to get into God's presence and seek the face of Jesus. She would tell me to have the scriptures I was standing on ready, so when I got into that place with God, then I could pray them.

This is where a lot of Christians are missing it. Praying the Bible is vital, but so often they don't, and then they wonder why their prayers aren't answered. When they go into prayer, they talk the problem and not the answer. The Word is our answer.

My grandmother didn't pray for things she couldn't back up with God's Word. At the same time, if she could find it in the Bible, she could believe for it, and her prayers would come to pass in the most amazing ways.

Sylvia believed God would always supply every need and she often stood on Philippians 4:19, "My God shall supply all your need according to his riches in glory by Christ Jesus." One time in her younger years, she went into prayer and said, "Lord, I need some food for my family." This prayer set off an unusual chain of events. That day, unbeknownst to my grandmother, a woman down the road decided to clean out her freezer. She laid some frozen meat on her front porch and then went back into her house. A dog went by the porch, saw a roast, grabbed it in his mouth and ran off. But instead of eating it, that dog took it straight to my grandmother's back porch and laid it down. There wasn't even a tear in the packaging. When my grandmother opened the back door, there was the roast! She went shouting and dancing and saying, "Thank you Jesus, thank you Jesus!" all over the house because dinner had arrived.

There were also many practical prayers she prayed for her family. In addition to praying for my grandfather's salvation, she had to continually pray about his jobs. He would always quit and, through the years, had many different jobs. However, my grandmother stood on Matthew 21:22, "and all things, what-soever ye shall ask in prayer, believing, you shall receive," and prayed that my grandfather would stay at a job until he retired.

She prayed and prayed, and he finally got a job at the railroad. Even though he threatened to quit, he actually liked the job and kept the job until he retired.

My grandfather also had a bit of a temper and my grandmother was a little frightened of him when he would get mad at her or the children, so she would back off and start praying in the Spirit. And when the boys had done something Grandpa didn't like, and he would give them a whipping, my grandmother would pray the scripture Psalms 30:5: "For his anger endureth but a moment; in his favor is life: weeping may endure for a night, but joy cometh in the morning." God always took care of her and her children.

My grandmother also had amazing results when she was praying for properties. She walked many properties for people and prayed, and whoever she prayed for got their land. She based those prayers on scriptures in the book of Joshua (1:3, 6:2–5).

One time the church we belonged had split. A pastor who did not want the Holy Spirit to move had come into our Assembly of God church, so a group from the church found some property they felt would work for a new building. But when the land owner met Paul Hinton, the church member who was going to buy the land, the owner asked "Who is the property for?"

Brother Paul said, "It's for us to build a church on."

The owner said, "Then it's not for sale. And if it was for sale, I would not sell it to you because I do not want a church here."

So Brother Paul and his wife Opal, my grandmother, myself and several others all went to the property. My grandmother said, "Now we are going to march around this property seven times, and on the last time we are going to shout, "This is our property!" So we marched around seven times and on the seventh time around, we all started shouting, "This property is ours!" and we started dancing and thanking the Lord for our property.

Then Sister Opal said, "Okay, what are we going to name the church?"

We decided on Step of Faith church and, in no time, the man that owned the land called Brother Paul.

"I don't know why I'm selling you this land," the owner said, "but how much of it do you want?"

"All of it," Brother Paul said. It was about 30 acres. After Brother Paul and Opal bought the property, they donated two acres of it for the new church and Step of Faith was born.

Healing was another area my grandmother had tremendous faith for. Not only had numerous prayers for her family's health been answered, God did miracles when she prayed for others to be healed. Once a church member, Henry Tackett, who would start a new job on a Monday, broke his arm the Friday before. Well, Henry needed that arm to work! Sunday in church, Grandma Sylvia and another brother from the church prayed for him. All of a sudden, the man started taking off his splint and he was totally healed! Another time my grandmother prayed for Sammy Patterson, who had a thyroid goiter. After the service, they all walked out on the porch of the church, and Sammy spit up the goiter and was healed completely!

My grandmother didn't have much money, but she knew how to pray for what she desired, and God would supply in such unexpected ways! Once, when Step of Faith started, she had asked God for money to help with the building project. Soon after that, she heard about a meeting that was going to take place in a Nigerian Church in Floyd, Texas, about ten minutes from her home in Farmersville, and she and my mother and some other ladies wanted to help. Their job was to wave banners as all the buses arrived and then welcome everyone as they got off the buses. My grandmother did this like she did everything, joyfully and praying in the Spirit.

Somehow during the service, these ladies found out that my grandmother was the little redheaded woman that Brother Kenneth Hagin, now a prominent minister, had talked about in his books. So the ladies came up to my grandmother and said, "Can you lay hands and pray for me?" Of course, she could not wait to pray for them. She loved praying for anybody!

But then the women started giving her money. My grandmother said, "Oh no, no! You don't have to pay me to pray for you. It's my honor to pray for you."

But they said, "We want to bless the woman of God."

She still wouldn't take the money, so the ladies just started stuffing the money in her pockets.

As my mother and grandmother were driving home, my mother asked, "What have you been praying and believing for?"

She said, "I asked the Lord for money so I can give it to the church."

"Well," my mother said, "look in your pockets and let's see how much money the Lord blessed you with."

My grandmother counted it. Then she told my mother to stop the car so she could dance and shout and praise God for His faithfulness. It was almost $300.

The Lord once told my grandmother, "I will reveal mysteries if you stay in my presence." So she would, and stood on Jeremiah 33:3, "Call to me and I will answer you, and I will tell you great and mighty things, which you do not know."

During the 40s, my grandmother and several other ladies were all a part of a prayer group. After their pastor, Brother Hagin, had taught on the gifts of the Spirit, they asked him if they could pray ask God for a word of knowledge about something. There was a woman in the church who, before she was a Christian, had her 16-year-old daughter disappear. The police thought, because the girl was involved with a motorcycle gang they were closing in on, perhaps the gang had killed her to keep her from giving too much information if she was arrested. They had even dragged the city lake, but never found her body. Others thought the motorcycle gang had kidnapped her when they left town. Either way she was never heard from again.

My Grandma Sylvia (in the middle) with her sisters Ava (left), and Ina (right). Circa 1914.

Circa 1918. From the left, Katherine, Sylvia, Ava, and Ina Kimberlin. My grandmother had one other younger sister, Marie, not pictured here.

Grandma Sylvia pictured in the middle of her daughters in 1995. From the left, Rosie, Joyce (my mother), Deloris, Shirley, and Carol.

Grandma Sylvia's granddaughters in 1994. From left, Toni, Marilyn, me, Tammy, Linda Sue, Sharon (and her baby Eli), Crystal, Gay Nell, Kim, Lois, Tina, Sherry (and her little girl Trease), and my sister Annette up front.

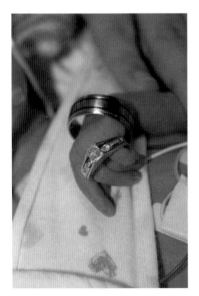 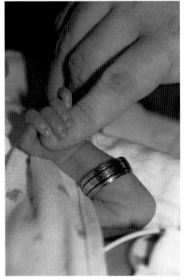

Pictures of my miracle granddaughter Kylie wearing her dad's wedding ring after she was born prematurely in December 23, 2013. Kylie is healthy and active today because of the power of prayer.

At Brother Hagin's Campmeetings Tulsa, OK, in 1991. Grandma Sylvia, me and my daughter Rebecca, my mom Joyce Bagwill, and Sister Joyce Mitchell.

My mom and grandmother with Brother and Sister Hagin at that same campmeeting.

Grandma Sylvia in 2000.

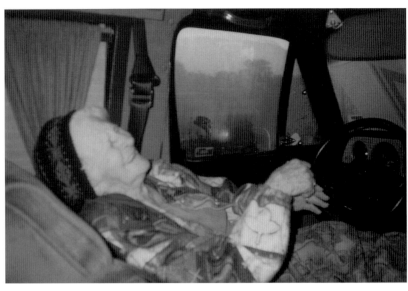

My grandmother laughing while camping at Brother Copeland's 1995 motorcycle rally in Texas. This is always how I remember my grandmother. So full of joy!

My Grandma Sylvia at the piano, circa 1949.

The Assemblies of God church in Farmersville, TX, that was my grandmother's
spiritual home for 67 years. Amazing things happened
among this congregation. This is the church in the mid 1940s,
while Brother Kenneth Hagin was pastor.

My grandmother (right) and her prayer partner, Sylvia Smith.

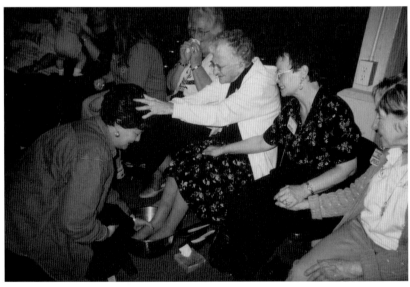

A footwashing ceremony at church in 2001. In her typical style, my grandmother was praying for a woman, Becky Sparks, who was trying to minister to her! Grandma Sylvia prayed for people every opportunity she got.

My favorite picture of my grandmother, circa 1998.

My grandmother never stopped "getting drunk" in the Spirit.
Here she was at 88, still drinking deeply! That's Kathy Kopal holding her
hand. I am right in front of her with my hand around my niece,
Amanda Voirin, drunk in the Spirit, and my sister Tammy is behind Grandma.
I learned how to drink with the best!

This is my family. In the back, my husband Rick and I (on the left) and my parents Joyce and Harold Bagwill. Front left is my youngest daughter Rachel, her husband Jacob, and their son Rayden (Guzman); Front right side is my oldest daughter Rebecca, her husband Jason, their son Jeraden and their daughter Kylie (Hogan).

My grandchildren Kylie, Rayden, and Jeraden.

Most everyone assumed the girl was dead. It had been 23 years, but the girl's mother, now a Christian, felt in her spirit that her daughter was alive, so she asked the prayer group if they'd mind praying and asking God about it. They, in turn, asked the pastor what he thought.

"Couldn't God give us a word of knowledge?" They asked the pastor. He told them he sure might, so they started praying and during a prayer meeting, there were tongues and interpretation and my grandmother saw in the Spirit that the woman was alive. My grandma also said by interpretation that, within 30 days, the mother would hear from her daughter.

Some of the people in the church who were not a part of the prayer group went to Brother Hagin and told him to stop them from praying for that lady's daughter. "That woman is dead, everybody knows that." But Brother Hagin said my grandmother was the most spiritual person in the church, and he trusted her interpretation. He told those people he wasn't going to stop them from praying. "Besides," he told them, "All you have to do is wait 30 days anyway to see if it comes to pass."

Well it did come to pass, and the daughter got in touch with her mom and eventually they were able to reunite. Another prayer answered.

$$\left(7\right)$$

The Power of Prayer
Continues On

The prayer secrets that I've learned from Grandma Sylvia have served me and my family well. No matter what the enemy has tried to hit us with, we have come back at him with scripture and prayer, and God has always made a way, all the glory be to him!

The key is what our grandma taught us, to know what the Bible says about everything so when things come up in our lives, we would know how to pray. You have to know what your authority is before you can speak it. This is something I've seen work over and over again. It is what I live by.

Six months before I turned 17 years old, my cousin and I were in a bad car wreck. I remember having a really hard time breathing, but I could hear Grandma Sylvia's voice saying, "You are healed, you are healed in Jesus' name," so that's what I started saying; "I'm healed in Jesus' name!"

A woman in the car behind us saw the accident and stopped to see if she could help. Thankfully she was a pastor, and she started praying in the Spirit, and so did I. By the time the paramedics arrived, I was talking to them about the Lord and telling jokes. My cousin was upset because she knew I was really hurt. I knew that too, but I also knew I was healed!

They took us to the hospital and ran x-rays on me. I had four cracked vertebrae. Then they started measuring me for a brace and said I was going to have to wear the brace for a whole year. I told them no, I wasn't going to wear a brace because I was healed in Jesus' name. Of course, they just looked and me and thought I was in denial.

Then I told them I'd have to be out of the hospital by the next day because I had church. This time they laughed. "You won't be out by tomorrow. It will take about a week for the brace to be even come in, and you have to have that before you can even leave."

"I am not missing church," I told them. My grandma never missed church, so I was not going to miss either!

Sunday morning I told them I wanted another x-ray so I could leave and go to church. After a while, they finally said they would do one, but there was no way I was going to be better. All the way down to the x-ray room, I said "Lord, I am speaking 1

Peter 2:24, and by Jesus stripes I am healed. You bore my sickness on the cross, and I am believing for total healing in Jesus name!"

Afterward, a doctor came in and said, "We don't know what is going on, but your vertebrae are already mending! It looks like you won't need the brace after all." Then they released me in time to make it to church!

I couldn't stay the whole service, but I stayed long enough for Grandma Sylvia and some of the ladies to lay hands on me. I knew that I had nothing to worry about because if Grandma prayed over me, then my healing would be complete, and I was.

Another time, my dad developed a knot on his neck and, after a while, it started to bother him. I took him to the doctor to check it out. After some tests, the doctor diagnosed him with stage four Non-Hodgkin Lymphoma. The doctor said it was a fast-spreading kind and that my father should start chemotherapy. My dad was fine with that, but he was also believing God for a miracle.

We found the scriptures we needed to be speaking over him like 1 Peter 2:24 (By Jesus stripes we are healed), and the Psalm 107:20 (He sent His word and healed them, and rescued them from their destruction), and Matthew 18:18 (Whatever you bind on earth will be bound in heaven, and whatever you loose on earth will be loosed in heaven).

Grandma Sylvia always said that when you speak the scriptures over a circumstance, always remember to thank the Lord and start praising Him for it like it is already done, so that is what we did. Based on the scriptures we found, we said, "We bind this cancer and command it to dry up at the root. No cancer can live in this body! We declare and decree Harold (my dad) will live and not die but declare the works of the Lord, and we thank you for it, Father. We praise you!"

After about his fifth treatment, the doctor did another scan to see how everything was doing. The doctor told my dad that whatever he was doing, it had worked. He no longer had cancer.

My dad told him that it was the power of prayer, and we all began to thank the Lord, dancing and praising God, just like Grandma said to do. Years later, he is still cancer free and doing great.

Healing is one of the promises of God, but so is protection, and that is another prayer we've prayed many times! One of the most memorable was on the night after Christmas in 2015, and it was stormy outside, and the wind was howling. We lost our electricity and there was a tornado coming. My mother Joyce and I were in the bathroom praying when we felt a big wind in the bathroom even thought there were no windows! We started rebuking the storm. Meanwhile, my husband and dad were out on the back porch watching the tornado. My husband was rebuking it and saying, "No, you cannot come near us! I command you to go back in the sky right now in the name of Jesus!"

My husband later told me that the Lord told him to speak and He would send His Spirit of light to move the storm. So when my husband spoke, a strong wind out of the north came out of nowhere and pushed the storm a quarter of a mile east of our house, then the wind stopped immediately.

We found out later that same tornado had hit some of the houses in our hometown before it hit Rowlett, Texas as an EF4. Several people died. Thank God we knew how to pray, or we might have been some of those killed.

Probably one of the most satisfying parts of prayer is watching it work in the lives of my children. When my daughter Rachel had my grandson, we had all prayed, and it was so peaceful. After she had him, they put him on her chest, but then the nurse quickly took him and said she needed to stimulate him. She took him over to the corner of the room. We didn't understand. We wanted to follow her to take some pictures of him, but the nurse told us no, that we couldn't go over there.

All of a sudden, the Lord told me to say, "I refuse to fear." So I did. I opened up my mouth and started to speak. Out loud I said, "We refuse to fear. He is a covenant child. No harm will come nigh him." My daughter Rachel started speaking in tongues and binding any fear.

"He is not breathing," a nurse said and they hit the code blue button. Nurses and doctors ran in and started working on him, and I said "I come against the spirit of death and fear in the name of Jesus!"

Meanwhile my daughter Rachel remained calm. Her husband said to her, "Why aren't you afraid? Look what is happening!"

"We are in covenant with God," Rachel said, "and our son is a covenant child, and no harm will come nigh him. "

"You have to speak the Word over this situation," I told my son-in-law. "Refuse to fear and speak, 'he will live and not die but declare the works of the Lord.'"

Then the Lord told him to get into agreement with the Word, so he said, "My son *will* live and not die! I refuse to fear!"

Immediately, my grandson started breathing, and to this day, he is in perfect health.

My other daughter, Rebecca, also came through a difficult birth with my granddaughter Kylie. When Rebecca was seven months pregnant with her, she woke up in the middle of the night, bleeding really badly. She had gone into early labor. My husband and I picked her and her husband up and brought them to the hospital, speaking the Word over Rebecca the entire trip. Rebecca was completely calm the whole time, but her husband was a little concerned.

When they checked her at the hospital, she wasn't dilated at all, but after about an hour, the contractions were getting really bad. I got the doctor and when she checked her again, Rebecca had dilated from 0 to 10, so they said they'd have to do a C-section. At the mention of a C-section, fear hit both me and her husband. Rebecca noticed.

"I need you both to get out of fear right now," she said passionately. "Start speaking wholeness. We are a covenant children and the Lord assured me the baby and I will be fine. Now are you in agreement with me?"

"Yes ma'am!" I said.

Kylie only weighed 2 lbs., 15 oz., but she was completely fine. They put an oxygen tube on her, but she never even had to use it. Of course Rebecca was fine too.

I was so impressed and amazed regarding my daughter, because through it all, she had so much faith. But I shouldn't have been surprised. She had been with me in every prayer meeting and every time I had gone to grandma's house. She had witnessed not only how my husband and I prayed, but how her great-grandmother prayed.

So not only did Grandma Sylvia leave a legacy to her children and my generation, but I also see it in my two daughters. Even as early as the age of three, if someone was hurt or sick, my daughters would pray. By that age, both of them had asked Jesus into their hearts and received their prayer language. Now they are both in the ministry with my husband and me. Rebecca and her husband are our associate pastors and worship leaders. Rachel and her husband are our youth pastors.

And now I see our prayers coming to pass in *my* grandchildren. My oldest grandchild Jeraden, who is 5, and his sister Kylie, almost 4, love to pray in the Spirit and lay hands on people. She even pretends she is preaching and singing. My grandson, was three when he asked Jesus into his heart, and my youngest granddaughter at almost two had begun to pray, and it sounds like she is praying in the Spirit. The same anointing that was on my grandma has and will continue to pass down from generation to generation. And I know, without a doubt that my grandchildren will also be in ministry, just like my daughters and their husbands.

(8)

Grandma Sylvia's Refrigerator Scriptures

Ever since I can remember, Grandma Sylvia always had scripture verses hanging all over her refrigerator. Some of them were from her Promise Box. These were individual verses printed on small rectangular pieces of paper that meant something to her. She also had several verses handwritten on pieces of notebook paper (or any other paper she could find when she needed it) and held in place by various magnets she had collected through the years.

In a way, her refrigerator was like a big prayer journal. The first thing she did every morning when she went into the kitchen was go to the refrigerator. Then she'd lay her hands on those scriptures and say them out loud, often praying out the Word she read. Many of the scriptures on the refrigerator changed throughout the years because when the Lord answered a prayer, she would remove the scripture she had been standing on and add new ones for new prayers she was believing for.

This is the list of scriptures Grandma Sylvia had on her refrigerator before she died. I've included them here because I think they tell a lot about why she trusted God and what she trusted Him for. I also think they'd be a great blessing for anybody to meditate on if they want to get closer to God.

Genesis 1:26–28

And God said, Let us make man in our image, after our likeness: and let them have dominion over the fish of the sea, and over the fowl of the air, and over the cattle, and over all the earth, and over every creeping thing that creepeth upon the earth.

So God created man in his own image, in the image of God created he him; male and female created he them.

And God blessed them, and God said unto them, Be fruitful, and multiply, and replenish the earth, and subdue it: and have dominion over the fish of the sea, and over the fowl of the air, and over every living thing that moveth upon the earth.

Deuteronomy 8:18

But thou shalt remember the Lord thy God: for it is he that giveth thee power to get wealth, that he may establish his covenant which he sware unto thy fathers, as it is this day.

Deuteronomy 28:13

And the Lord shall make thee the head, and not the tail, and thou shalt be above only, and thou shalt not be beneath; if that thou hearken unto the commandments of the Lord thy God, which I command thee this day, to observe and to do them:

1 Samuel 5:1–3

And the Philistines took the ark of God, and brought it from Ebenezer unto Ashdod. When the Philistines took the ark of God, they brought it into the house of Dagon, and set it by Dagon. And when they of Ashdod arose early on the morrow, behold, Dagon was fallen upon his face to the earth before the ark of the Lord. And they took Dagon, and set him in his place again.

1 Kings 8:56

Blessed be the Lord that hath given rest unto his people Israel, according to all that he promised: there hath not failed one word of all his good promise, which he promised by the hand of Moses his servant.

Psalm 37:4

Delight thyself also in the Lord: and he shall give thee the desires of thine heart.

Psalm 103:1–4

Bless the Lord, O my soul: and all that is within me, bless his holy name. Bless the Lord, O my soul, and forget not all his benefits: Who forgiveth all thine iniquities; who healeth all thy diseases;

Who redeemeth thy life from destruction; who crowneth thee with lovingkindness and tender mercies;

Psalm 145:16

Thou openest thine hand, and satisfies the desire of every living thing.

Psalm 145:17–19

The Lord is righteous in all his ways, and holy in all his works. The Lord is nigh unto all them that call upon him, to all that call upon him in truth. He will fulfil the desire of them that fear him: he also will hear their cry, and will save them.

Psalm 1:1-2

Blessed is the man that walketh not in the counsel of the ungodly, nor standeth in the way of sinners, nor sitteth in the seat of the scornful. But his delight is in the law of the Lord; and in his law doth he meditate day and night.

Proverbs 8:28–36

When he established the clouds above: when he strengthened the fountains of the deep:

When he gave to the sea his decree, that the waters should not pass his commandment: when he appointed the foundations of the earth:

Then I was by him, as one brought up with him: and I was daily his delight, rejoicing always before him;

Rejoicing in the habitable part of his earth; and my delights were with the sons of men.

Now therefore hearken unto me, O ye children: for blessed are they that keep my ways.

Hear instruction, and be wise, and refuse it not.

Blessed is the man that heareth me, watching daily at my gates, waiting at the posts of my doors.

For whoso findeth me findeth life, and shall obtain favour of the Lord.

But he that sinneth against me wrongeth his own soul: all they that hate me love death.

Proverbs 10:22–24

The blessing of the Lord, it maketh rich, and he addeth no sorrow with it.

It is as sport to a fool to do mischief: but a man of understanding hath wisdom.

The fear of the wicked, it shall come upon him: but the desire of the righteous shall be granted.

Proverbs 11:1–4

A false balance is abomination to the Lord: but a just weight is his delight.

When pride cometh, then cometh shame: but with the lowly is wisdom.

The integrity of the upright shall guide them: but the perverseness of transgressors shall destroy them.

Riches profit not in the day of wrath: but righteousness delivereth from death.

Proverbs 17:27

He that hath knowledge spareth his words: and a man of understanding is of an excellent spirit.

Proverbs 22: 7

The rich ruleth over the poor, and the borrower is servant to the lender.

Proverbs 22:19–22

That thy trust may be in the Lord, I have made known to thee this day, even to thee.

Have not I written to thee excellent things in counsels and knowledge,

That I might make thee know the certainty of the words of truth; that thou mightest answer the words of truth to them that send unto thee?

Rob not the poor, because he is poor: neither oppress the afflicted in the gate:

Proverbs 29:18

Where there is no vision, the people perish: but he that keepeth the law, happy is he.

Isaiah 66:7

Before she travailed, she brought forth; before her pain came, she was delivered of a man child.

Isaiah 58:14

Then shalt thou delight thyself in the Lord; and I will cause thee to ride upon the high places of the earth, and feed thee with the heritage of Jacob thy father: for the mouth of the Lord hath spoken it.

Joel 2:13, 17

And rend your heart, and not your garments, and turn unto the Lord your God: for he is gracious and merciful, slow to anger, and of great kindness, and repenteth him of the evil. . . . Let the priests, the ministers of the Lord, weep between the porch and the altar, and let them say, Spare thy people, O Lord, and give not thine heritage to reproach, that the heathen should rule over them: wherefore should they say among the people, Where is their God?

Joel 3:4–8

Yea, and what have ye to do with me, O Tyre, and Zidon, and all the coasts of Palestine? will ye render me a recompence? and if ye recompense me, swiftly and speedily will I return your recompence upon your own head;

Because ye have taken my silver and my gold, and have carried into your temples my goodly pleasant things:

The children also of Judah and the children of Jerusalem have ye sold unto the Grecians, that ye might remove them far from their border.

Behold, I will raise them out of the place whither ye have sold them, and will return your recompence upon your own head:

And I will sell your sons and your daughters into the hand of the children of Judah, and they shall sell them to the Sabeans, to a people far off: for the Lord hath spoken it.

Amos 9:13

Behold, the days come, saith the Lord, that the plowman shall overtake the reaper, and the treader of grapes him that soweth seed; and the mountains shall drop sweet wine, and all the hills shall melt.

Matthew 5:4–8

Blessed are they that mourn: for they shall be comforted. Blessed are the meek: for they shall inherit the earth. Blessed are they which do hunger and thirst after righteousness: for they shall be filled. Blessed are the merciful: for they shall obtain mercy. Blessed are the pure in heart: for they shall see God.

Matthew 10:2-4

These are the name of the twelve apostles: first, Simon (who is called Peter) and his brother Andrew; James son of Zebedee, and his brother John; Philip and Bartholomew; Thomas and Matthew the tax collector; James son of Alphaeus, and Thaddaeus; Simon the Zealot and Judas Iscariot, who betrayed him.

Matthew 12:5-7

Or have ye not read in the law, how that on the sabbath days the priests in the temple profane the sabbath, and are blameless? But I say unto you, That in this place is one greater than the temple. But if ye had known what this meaneth, I will have mercy, and not sacrifice, ye would not have condemned the guiltless.

Matthew 11:28-30

Come unto me, all ye that labour and are heavy laden, and I will give you rest. Take my yoke upon you, and learn of me; for I am meek and lowly in heart: and ye shall find rest unto your souls. For my yoke is easy, and my burden is light.

Matthew 12:36-37

But I say unto you, That every idle word that men shall speak, they shall give account thereof in the day of judgment. For by thy words thou shalt be justified, and by thy words thou shalt be condemned.

Matthew 16:19

And I will give unto thee the keys of the kingdom of heaven: and whatsoever thou shalt bind on earth shall be bound in heaven: and whatsoever thou shalt loose on earth shall be loosed in heaven.

PRAYER OF SALVATION

God loves you—no matter who you are, no matter what your past. God loves you so much that He gave His one and only begotten Son for you. The Bible tells us that "...whoever believes in Him shall not perish but have eternal life" (John 3:16 NIV). Jesus laid down His life and rose again so that we could spend eternity with Him in heaven and experience His absolute best on earth. If you would like to receive Jesus into your life, say the following prayer out loud and mean it from your heart.

Heavenly Father, I come to You admitting that I am a sinner. Right now, I choose to turn away from sin, and I ask You to cleanse me of all unrighteousness. I believe that Your Son, Jesus, died on the cross to take away my sins. I also believe that He rose again from the dead so that I might be forgiven of my sins and made righteous through faith in Him. I call upon the name of Jesus Christ to be the Savior and Lord of my life. Jesus, I choose to follow You and ask that You fill me with the power of the Holy Spirit. I declare that right now I am a child of God. I am free from sin and full of the righteousness of God. I am saved in Jesus' name. Amen.

If you prayed this prayer to receive Jesus Christ as your Savior for the first time, please contact us on the Web at **www.harrisonhouse.com** to receive a free book.

Or you may write to us at

Harrison House • P.O. Box 35035 • Tulsa, Oklahoma 74153

The Harrison House Vision

Proclaiming the truth and the power

Of the Gospel of Jesus Christ

With excellence;

Challenging Christians to

Live victoriously,

Grow spiritually,

Know God intimately.

Fast. Easy.
Convenient.

For the latest Harrison House product information and author news, look no further than your computer. All the details on our powerful, life-changing products are just a click away. New releases, E-mail subscriptions, testimonies, monthly specials — find it all in one place. Visit harrisonhouse.com today!

harrisonhouse